My State

PENNSYLVANIA

By Christina Earley

TABLE OF CONTENTS

A Crabtree Seedlings Book

Crabtree Publishing

crabtreebooks.com

School-to-Home Support for Caregivers and Teachers

This book helps children grow by letting them practice reading. Here are a few guiding questions to help the reader build his or her comprehension skills. Possible answers appear in red.

Before Reading:

- What do I know about Pennsylvania?
    - *I know that Pennsylvania is a state.*
    - *I know that there is a chocolate factory in Pennsylvania.*

- What do I want to learn about Pennsylvania?
    - *I want to learn which famous people were born in Pennsylvania.*
    - *I want to learn what the state flag looks like.*

During Reading:

- What have I learned so far?
    - *I have learned that Harrisburg is the state capital of Pennsylvania.*
    - *I have learned that the first public celebration of George Washington's birthday was at Valley Forge.*

- I wonder why...
    - *I wonder why the state flower is the mountain laurel.*
    - *I wonder why there are so many bridges in Pittsburgh.*

After Reading:

- What did I learn about Pennsylvania?
    - *I have learned that you can dogsled at the Pocono Mountains.*
    - *I have learned that the state animal is the white-tailed deer.*

- Read the book again and look for the glossary words.
    - *I see the word **capital** on page 6, and the word **caverns** on page 21. The other glossary words are found on pages 22 and 23.*

PENNSYLVANIA
Hi! My name is Emma. Welcome to Pennsylvania!

I live in Pittsburgh. There are more than 400 bridges here.

My city is where Heinz ketchup was created.

Pennsylvania is in the northeastern United States. The **capital** is Harrisburg.

Fun Fact: Philadelphia is the largest city in Pennsylvania.

The state animal is the white-tailed deer.

The mountain laurel is the state flower.

We grow a lot of cherries. Some of them are used to make my favorite dessert, cherry pie!

Fun Fact: Pennsylvania has more than 1 million cherry trees.

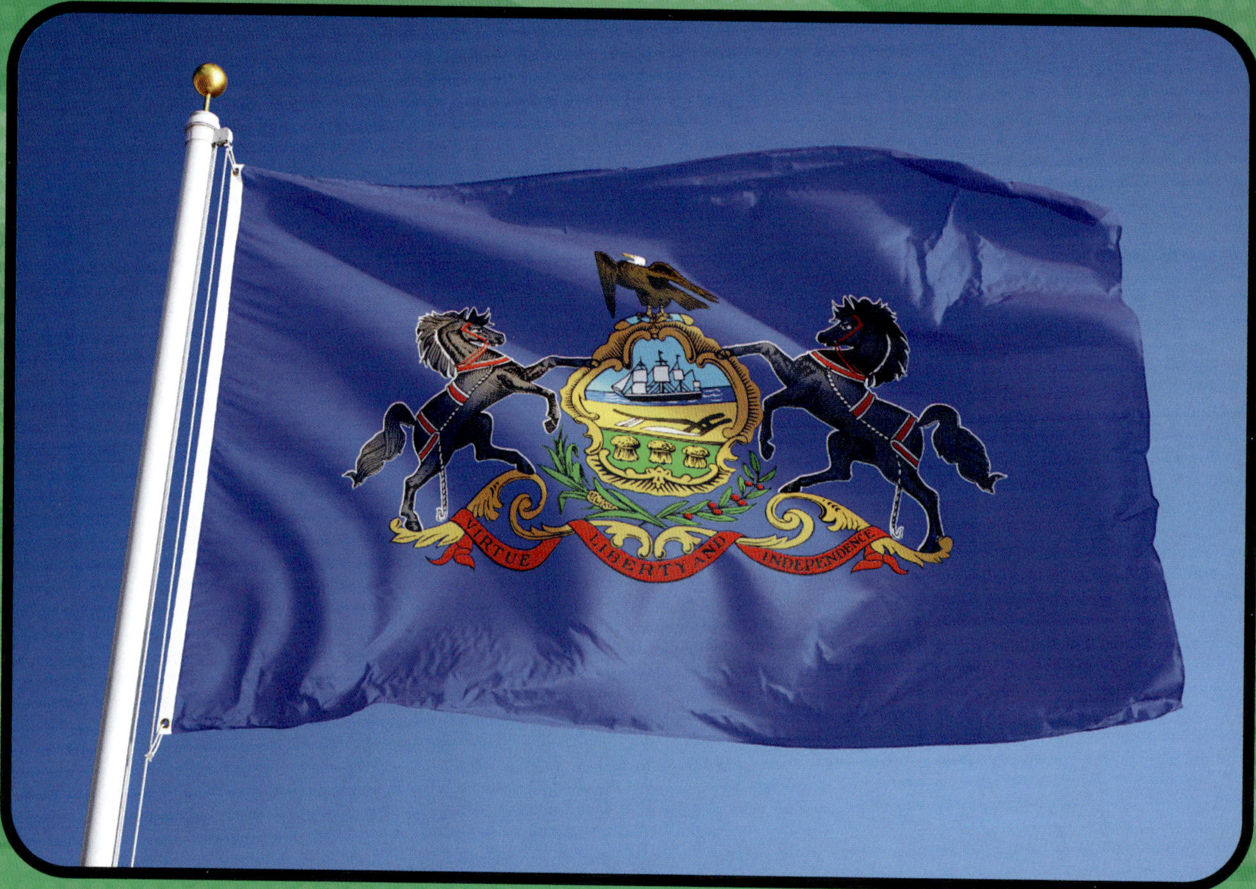

My state flag is blue. The state **coat of arms** is in the middle.

There are eight national sports teams in Pennsylvania.

NAKED AND STARVING AS THEY ARE
WE CANNOT ENOUGH ADMIRE
THE INCOMPARABLE PATIENCE AND FIDELITY
OF THE SOLDIERY

I like to visit Valley Forge National Historical Park. I pretend I am in the **Continental Army**. It was led by George Washington.

Fun Fact: The first public celebration of Washington's birthday was at Valley Forge in 1778.

I make my own candy bar at Hersheypark.

I go **dogsledding** in the Pocono Mountains.

Singer Taylor Swift was born in Pennsylvania. NBA **shooting guard** Kobe Bryant was also born in Pennsylvania.

Fun Fact: President Joe Biden was born in Scranton, Pennsylvania.

I like to go boating on Lake Nockamixon.
3901

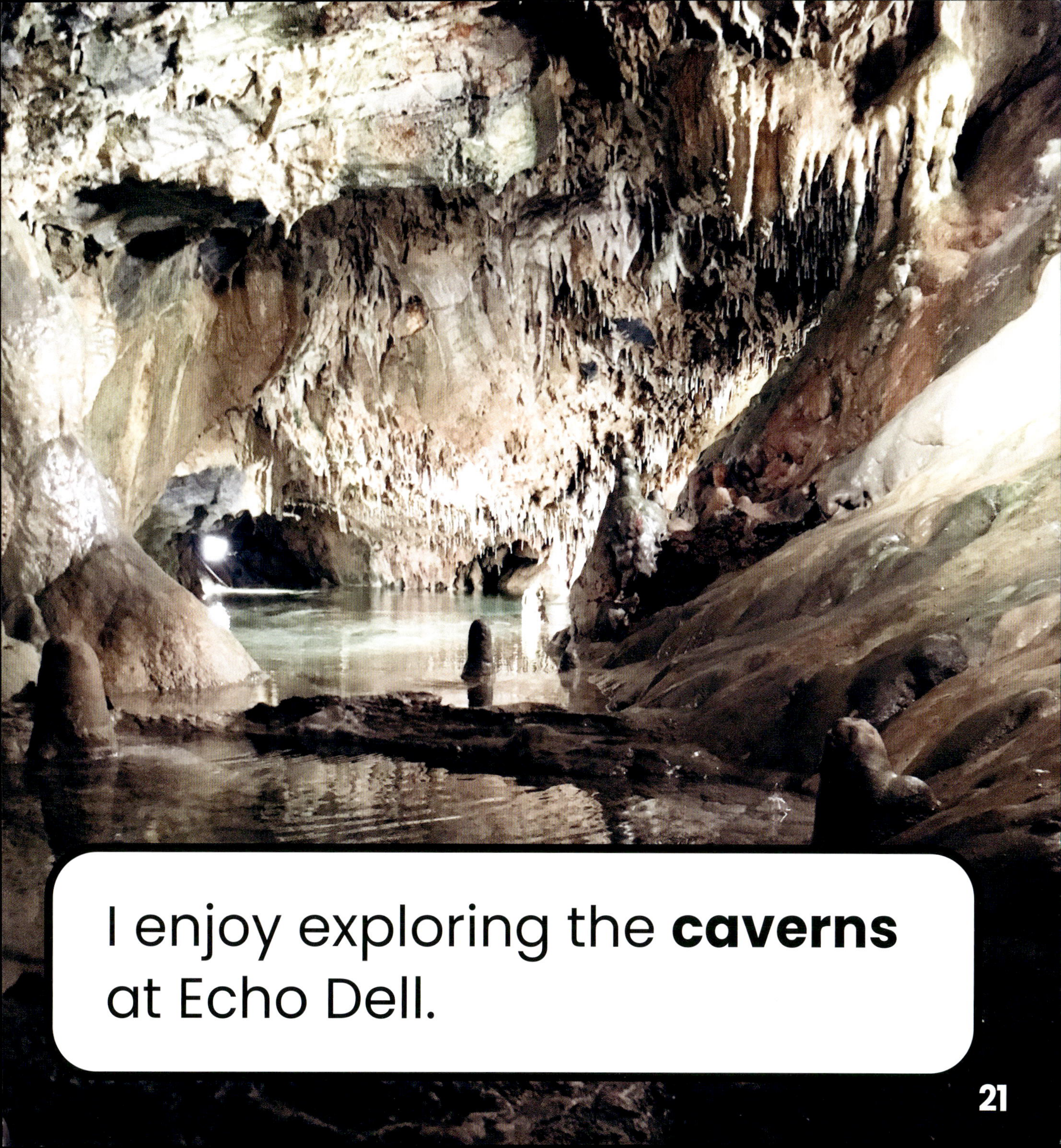

I enjoy exploring the **caverns** at Echo Dell.

Glossary

capital (cap-ih-tuhl): The city or town where the government of a country, state, or province is located

caverns (kav-ernz): Large caves, usually underground

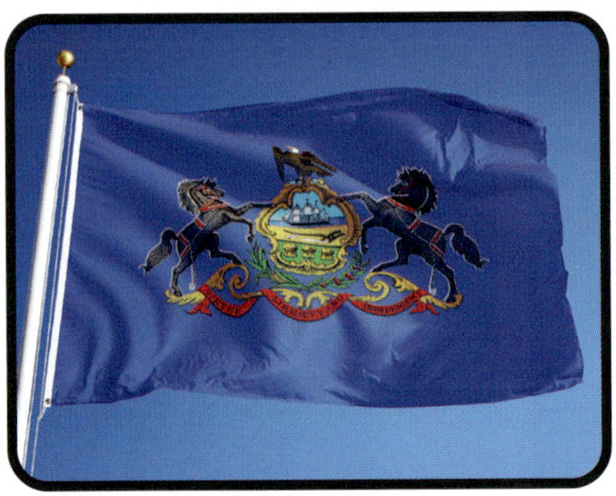

coat of arms (coht uv armz): A special group of pictures, usually shown on a shield

Continental Army (kon-tin-en-tuhl ar-mee): The colonial army that fought against the British in the American Revolutionary War

dogsledding (dawg-slehd-ing): To travel in a type of sled that is pulled by dogs

shooting guard (shoo-ting gard): A position on a basketball team

Index

About the Author

Christina Earley lives in sunny South Florida with her husband and son. She enjoys traveling around the United States and learning about different historical places. Her hobbies include hiking, yoga, and baking.

Written by: Christina Earley
Designed and Illustrated by: Bobbie Houser
Series Development: James Earley
Proofreader: Melissa Boyce
Educational Consultant: Marie Lemke M.Ed.

Photographs:
Alamy: Gene Lower: p. 18 right, 23; IanDagnall Computing: p. 19
Shutterstock: Harold Stiver: cover; Jon Bilous: p. 3; Tupungato: p. 4; JJava Designs: p. 5; Volina: p. 6, 22; f11photo: p. 7; Paul Tessier: p. 8; EQRoy: p. 9; overcrew: p. 10-11; Alena Levykin: p. 11; railway fx: p. 12, 22; Jai Agnish: p. 13; Delmas Lehman: p. 14-15, 23; Rosemarie Mosteller: p. 15; Alizada Studios: p. 16; COLOMBO NICOLA: p. 17, 23; Brian Friedman: p. 18 left; Christian Carollo: p. 20; Amy R. Gillung: p. 21, 22

Crabtree Publishing

crabtreebooks.com 800-387-7650

Printed in the U.S.A./012023/CG20220815

Published in Canada
Crabtree Publishing
616 Welland Avenue
St. Catharines, Ontario
L2M 5V6

Published in the United States
Crabtree Publishing
347 Fifth Avenue
Suite 1402-145
New York, New York, 10016

Library and Archives Canada Cataloguing in Publication
Available at Library and Archives Canada

Library of Congress Cataloging-in-Publication Data
Available at the Library of Congress

Hardcover: 978-1-0396-9660-0
Paperback: 978-1-0396-9767-6
Ebook (pdf): 978-1-0396-9981-6
Epub: 978-1-0396-9874-1